The FIRST BOOK of
THE CHINA CLIPPERS

Other books by Louise Dickinson Rich

THE FIRST BOOK OF THE EARLY SETTLERS
THE FIRST BOOK OF NEW ENGLAND
THE FIRST BOOK OF NEW WORLD EXPLORERS
THE FIRST BOOK OF THE VIKINGS

The clipper ships had an almost unbelievable beauty.

The FIRST BOOK of

THE CHINA
CLIPPERS

★ ★ ★ ★ ★ ★ ★ ★

Louise Dickinson Rich

PICTURES BY *Henry S. Gillette*

FRANKLIN WATTS, INC.
575 Lexington Avenue, New York 22

FIRST PRINTING
Library of Congress Catalog Card Number: 62–14072
© Copyright 1962 by Louise Dickinson Rich
Printed in the United States of America

Foreword

Almost everyone finds, in thinking over his life, that one time
stands out above all others as particularly interesting and exciting. Each country, too, seems to have in its history an era of
romance and adventure, unusually full of color and courage
and glory. For England, it may have been the time of King
Arthur's court; for the Scandinavian countries, the Viking Age;
for Greece, the half-mythical years when Jason sought the
Golden Fleece and Theseus killed the Minotaur. For our own
country it may well have been the brilliant era of the clipper
ships, the heroic days of the China trade.

The heyday of the clippers came in the thirty years just before the Civil War, reaching its peak in the 1850's. During
these years, the art of building wooden sailing vessels came near
to perfection. Dreaming always of greater speed, ship designers
and shipwrights became more and more daring and departed
further and further from the safe old ideas of proper line and
construction. At first accidentally and then with forethought,
these men achieved an almost unbelievable beauty in the tall
ships that came off the ways. Even today these ships are considered among the loveliest works ever created by man's hand.

The swift, sensitive ships had beautiful names, too: *Shoot-
ing Star*, *Wild Wave*, *Morning Light*, *White Squall*, and perhaps the most famous of them all, *Flying Cloud*. All over the

v

world these names were familiar not only to those who followed the sea, but to everyday people who lived out their lives on the land, as well. And all over America the ships' records were as well known to townsmen and farmers and schoolteachers and carpenters as the records of major league baseball teams are today. The progress of each clipper in the tea race from China (or, later on, in the voyage to California) was watched as closely and intensely as the World Series is now. Each ship had its loyal fans, and many a bet was won or lost on the outcome of the races.

But the clippers did more than transport merchandise and provide a sporting event for bystanders. They opened up a new way of life for a great many people—a way sometimes hard and dangerous, sometimes almost fabulous, and always various and exciting. By means of the clippers, men and women who might otherwise have lived narrow, small-town lives broadened their horizons to include the whole world, and found richness and wisdom and understanding of other peoples and other ways of life. With the aid of these ships and their officers, the mysteries of the winds and ocean currents were studied and a whole new science was born. The clippers even brought about changes in English laws that had been unquestioned for two centuries. Going about their business at the far ends of the earth, the Yankee clippers stood for much more than dollars and cents.

The tall ships, with all their rushing life and beauty under sail, are gone now. No longer can little boys name in order the canvases of a full-rigged three-master, from foresail, mainsail, and crossjack all the way up through topgallant, royal, skysail, and moonraker. Very few men still live who remember the frozen horror of beating around Cape Horn, with its mountainous seas and howling gales, or the tense watches in the Java Sea, when at any moment a fleet of *praus* manned by fierce Malayan pirates might swarm out from behind a headland and attack the ship. Over a hundred years have passed since the *Sea Witch* astonished the world by sailing home from China to New York in seventy-seven days to set a record that was broken only by herself on a later voyage.

Who planned these ships, and who built them? What kind of men captained them and manned them? How did the crews live during the long months at sea? What did they see and do when they arrived at last in China? What did they bring home with them? What was there about the China trade that appeals so much to the imagination?

Those are the questions to which we shall try to find answers.

Contents

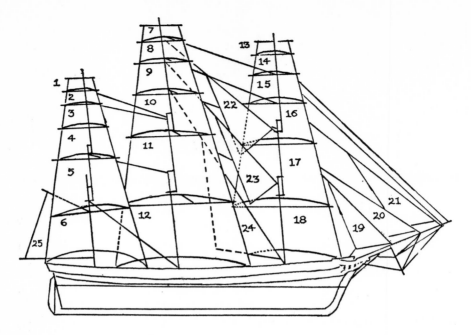

Sail plan of a clipper ship:

1. Mizzen skysail
2. Mizzen royal
3. Mizzen topgallant sail
4. Upper mizzen topsail
5. Lower mizzen topsail
6. Mizzen sail (crossjack)
7. Main skysail
8. Main royal
9. Main topgallant sail
10. Upper main topsail
11. Lower main topsail
12. Mainsail
13. Fore skysail
14. Fore royal
15. Fore topgallant sail
16. Upper fore topsail
17. Lower fore topsail
18. Foresail
19. Inner jib
20. Outer jib
21. Flying jib
22. Main royal staysail
23. Main topgallant staysail
24. Main topmast staysail

25. Spanker

Staysails could also be fitted to the fore- and mizzenmasts; and, in a light wind, a moonsail or moonraker—a square sail—was set above a skysail on some clipper ships.

1

Before the Clippers

To understand how the China trade came about and why the clipper ships were necessary, we must go back in history to colonial times, when no American shipmaster even thought about going to the Orient. Trade between the English-speaking countries and the Far East was recognized as belonging exclusively to the British East India Company, and nobody dreamed of interfering. This company, sometimes called the "John Company," was established in 1600. Over the years, the company had grown so rich and powerful that it held a true monopoly on the Eastern trade and controlled the lives of millions of people, both at home and in India and China. It was much too big and strong for the little colonial merchant marine to tackle in a trade war.

Actually, the colonists had no need or wish to expand their shipping. They were doing very well with a profitable business which they had built up in the Atlantic, in molasses, rum, and slaves. On this three-cornered trade many old and respected

American fortunes were based. This is the way it worked. Ships from New England and some other ports sailed to the coast of Africa, where as many Negroes as possible were purchased or kidnapped. These unfortunates were battened down in the holds of the vessels for a long, unhappy trip back across the Atlantic to the West Indies. There they were sold to the owners of the sugar plantations. The ship was loaded with sugar and molasses and sailed along the third side of the triangle, back to New England, where the cargo was mostly made into rum. This was sold locally, or sent along to Africa where it was traded for more slaves. When the South began to raise cotton and tobacco in increasing quantities, the demand for slave labor grew, and the three-cornered trade boomed.

Oddly enough, many of the people engaged in it were extremely pious. Often in old bills of lading there are entries such as this: "Twenty hogsheads of rum, shipped by the Grace of God in the good sloop *Cletis*, bound by God's Grace for the coast of Guinea." No one seemed concerned that the rum would be traded for human beings. Round and round the triangle the ships went, piling up money on every trip. Money seemed reason enough for this cruel traffic.

By no means all the colonial ships carried rum and slaves, however. There was a large fishing fleet that did a thriving business, selling the catches at home and abroad. And many other boats transported general cargoes of grain, cotton, lumber, tobacco, furs, and sundry other goods up and down the coast and overseas to Europe. There was enough trade near home to keep everyone occupied without dashing off to the Pacific, a long and difficult voyage at best.

The slaves were sold to the owners of sugar plantations.

Then came the American Revolution. When it was over, America found herself free and independent of England; she also found that her shipping was in a bad way. During the war, since at the time America had only the beginnings of a navy, many vessels had served as warships. And it had been almost impossible for the others to carry on trade, even along their own coast. Sea-lanes had been policed and ports blockaded by British ships. Although some blockade-running and smuggling had been done, commerce had suffered greatly. A new start, almost from scratch, would have to be made by the infant nation.

The loss of vessels through sinking or capture was not too serious. From the beginning, Americans had been expert builders of ships. In the shipyards that lined the coast from Maryland to Maine, the fleet could be restored. Where to send the new vessels was the problem. The British now barred the West Indies to all but their own shipping; this put an end to the rum-molasses-and-slave trade. Furthermore, according to the old English Navigation Laws of 1651, no foreign ships— and American ships were now foreign—were allowed to trade with any of the many British possessions. This left the new American merchant marine in the position of being all dressed up with almost no place to go; or at least, none of the old, familiar places. The only answer was to find new markets, and the logical place to find them was in the Orient.

With this idea in mind, Captain John Green sailed the *Empress of China* from New York in 1784 on the first direct voyage ever made by an American ship to Canton. China was only a name to the people of the United States, and even the highly civilized Chinese nobility, perhaps the most cultured people in the world of the day, knew nothing of the struggling new nation on the far shore of North America. But the great merchant princes in their silk robes and black skullcaps showed a lively interest in the foreign ship with the unknown flag. They welcomed Captain Green warmly, seeing in him the promise of a fine new market for their tea and silks. When he sailed for home, his holds were crammed with a rich cargo which sold at once at a tremendous profit. The report of Samuel Shaw, the supercargo, or bookkeeper and clerk, aboard the *Empress*, was read in Congress. It attracted a great deal of attention and all along the coast it turned the thoughts of shipowners to the East.

Among the ships that were fitted out for the China trade was the *Columbia*. Accompanied by the sloop *Lady Washington*, which was captained by Robert Gray, it sailed from Boston around Cape Horn in 1787. Once in the Pacific, the two ships detoured to the northwest coast of America to barter with the Indians for furs, which the shipowners rightly supposed would find a good market in the Orient. With sufficient furs to make a cargo, the *Columbia* went on to Canton in 1789, with Captain Gray in command. Because of the monsoons—the seasonal winds of the South Pacific, which blow steadily from the southwest in summer and from the northeast in winter—Gray returned to Boston with his valuable cargo of Chinese goods by a different route, around the Cape of Good Hope, in Africa. Thus on his voyage he did two outstanding things: he established another three-cornered trade route between the United States, the fur coast, and China; and he became the first American to circumnavigate the globe.

On his next voyage in the *Columbia*, in 1792, Captain Gray explored the northwest coast more thoroughly. Among his important discoveries was a great river which he called the Columbia, after his ship. Through this discovery, Gray gave to the United States a valid claim to all the immense territory later explored by Lewis and Clark.

Going to out-of-the-way places and making strange discoveries was by no means unusual to those engaged in the China trade. Trading with China involved more than merely sailing from New York or Boston to Canton and back again. In order to have healthy trade relations, it was necessary to have something to offer besides money—some form of merchandise needed or wanted by the trading country. In China, the demand for furs —sea otter, at first—was great and constant. Before they headed for China, Americans went first to where the sea otter were.

For a while, after the voyages of the *Columbia*, sea otter pelts were found in abundance among the Indians along the northwest coast of America. After some years, however, so great was the slaughter that fur pelts became scarce. It was no longer worth while to trade for them in the Northwest. In the meantime, however, American traders had found that the Chinese also liked sealskins. The rich sealing grounds were on the icy islands toward the region of the South Pole, and sealing expeditions headed for them.

In the meantime, the United States had engaged in another war with Great Britain, the War of 1812. This arose directly through differences of opinion on American rights at sea. England viewed with alarm American enterprise and energy in expanding trade, and did everything possible to discourage the young nation that was threatening British rule of the seas. American ports were again blockaded, and American ships were stopped at sea and searched for British seamen supposed to be aboard. If the British needed sailors, they often seized likely-looking Americans and forced them to serve. The war finally ended in 1814 with the signing of the Treaty of Ghent, and Americans were free to turn their whole attention to trade expansion.

It was during this war that one of the most celebrated of the later clipper-ship captains, Nathaniel Palmer, received his first lessons at sea. Nat was only a fourteen-year-old boy in Stonington, Connecticut, when the war broke out, but he shipped aboard a coastal vessel that slipped in and out of blockaded ports between New York and Maine, carrying necessities to the citizens whom the British were trying to starve into surrender. He stayed with the coastal ships until he was eighteen years old and an experienced hand at getting out of tight spots at sea.

When Captain James Sheffield of the brig *Hersilia* needed a second mate who could "smell his way through fog by night from Hellgate to Providence," he signed on Nat Palmer. The *Hersilia* was going to the southern arctic regions to look for seals, to an unknown and dangerous area full of uncharted reefs and great icebergs, tormented by howling winds and gigantic waves, and shrouded much of the time in dense fog. There, compasses often went crazy and instruments were useless in the sightless murk. A sailor needed a special instinct to guide him when everything else failed. Nat Palmer had that instinct.

He proved so competent and valuable a man that in 1820, when the fleet returned to the rich new sealeries they had found,

7

The British often seized American sailors.

Nat was Captain Palmer of the little sloop *Hero*, a shallow vessel used chiefly for scouting out new seal islands. He was twenty-one years old, and his first and second mates, Phineas Wilcox and Richard Loper, were about the same age. The common seamen were a sixteen-year-old boy, Stanton Burdick, and the Negro Peter Harvey, the old man of them all at the age of thirty-one. This little cockleshell of a boat and its youthful crew do not sound very impressive, or even very trustworthy to be sailing alone at the wild and lonely bottom of the world. Yet they discovered a new continent.

It happened this way. When the *Hersilia*, the *Hero*, and four other ships arrived at the South Shetland Islands where they had loaded nine thousand sealskins at five dollars apiece the year before, they found thirty other vessels already there. Very few seals were left, and the *Hero* was sent south to scout for new breeding grounds. The fleet could not afford to go home with empty holds.

Palmer headed for Deception Island, one of the South Shetlands. The next day was cloudy, and great banks and walls of fog streamed and twisted over the ice-clogged gray water. The *Hero* was forced to proceed slowly. Suddenly everyone aboard heard the voices of many birds—penguins, albatrosses, gulls, sea pigeons and shrill Mother Carey's chickens—and they knew that land must be close. Then through a rift in the fog they saw one of the strangest islands in the world. A high ring of ice-covered black rock curved around a big, calm bay, whose water steamed and bubbled. It was the partly submerged crater of a live volcano, whose deep fires kept the water hot in spite of the huge cakes of ice that dropped into it constantly from the gla-

9

A high ring of ice-covered rock curved around the bay.

ciers on the rim. Smoke and steam hissed from cracks in the rock, and occasionally an eerie rumbling rose from the bowels of the volcano. Outside the sheltering rock ring, surf thundered and icebergs crashed and groaned. Overhead, clouds of birds wheeled and cried in the drifting fog. It was a weird, unearthly place.

The crew of the *Hero* forgot for a while that they were responsible seamen. It had been a long time since any of them had been swimming or even had a hot bath. Like the boys they really were, they stripped and plunged into the warm water. They yelled and splashed and ducked each other, and had a wonderful time. Late in his life, when he had been to every corner of the globe and seen many strange sights, old Captain Palmer still remembered best and with most pleasure the day when the *Hero*'s crew had taken time off to go swimming at Deception Island.

Two days later, in November, 1820, Nat Palmer climbed a high peak on the island and saw far to the south a looming range of snow-clad mountains. No chart showed any such huge mass of land, but there it was, all the same. Still looking for seals, he headed south along the foggy, barren coast he had glimpsed. He saw no seal herds, and the icebound coast made landing difficult. But what he and his crew were viewing was a tremendous new continent. For many years it was marked Palmer Land on maps, and if a claim had been thought worth while, the United States could have made it by right of discovery. At the time, though, no one was interested in a frozen waste of ice and snow—since it had no seals. Finally the territory became known as Antarctica, and was claimed by England

and various other countries, although one long tongue of land is called Palmer Peninsula to this day.

The sealers were not the only ones to explore the far corners of the earth and to find and chart new lands. The whaling ships of Nantucket and New Bedford were probably even more familiar with the seven seas. To find seals, it was necessary to go where there was land on which they could rest and breed. But the whales and the whalers lumbered and wallowed back and forth over most of the watery world.

The crews of merchantmen and sealers rather looked down on whaling men. When they encountered one, they were likely to bawl out lines from one of their favorite sea chanteys:

> *Oh-oh, Ranzo was no sailor,*
> *So they shipped him aboard a whaler,*
> *Poor Reuben Ranzo!*

Actually, the whalers were excellent seamen, brave, tough, and resourceful. They had to be. They took voyages of two or three years' duration into the roughest and most treacherous seas, and they pursued in small boats the world's largest, trickiest mammals and fought them with light harpoons and lances. Often the fragile boats were splintered to kindling wood by infuriated whales, and the men were lost forever; and sometimes the mother ships themselves were rammed and sunk. Whaling was no occupation for the timid, the clumsy, or the weak.

But compared to the trim trading and sealing ships, with their scoured decks, scraped spars, white canvas, and taut rigging, the whaling vessels did look sloppy. It couldn't be

The fragile boats were often wrecked by infuriated whales.

helped. After the whale had been killed, it was tied up alongside the ship. The thick blubber was stripped off, thrown into a huge caldron, and boiled to extract the whale oil. The flesh was cut away for the valuable whalebone. For a while, the ship was turned into a factory and butchery. The decks and sides of the vessel swam in grease and blood, and oily smoke rose to smudge the sails. Little by little the whaler grew more and more slatternly and disreputable-looking, until she was an object of scorn to other ships.

There was money in this dirty and dangerous business, though. Whale oil for lamps, and bone for many manufactured articles were in big demand. The members of the crew signed on not for set wages, but for a share of the profits. On a successful voyage a man could make much more money than he would have on a cleaner, safer ship; and the thrill of gambling was added to the natural excitements of seafaring. The next voyage might make a man rich; and in the meantime, he enjoyed an adventurous, roving life.

Busy as the twenty years following the War of 1812 were for American shipping, they served in large part as preparation for a glorious time to come. During them, American seamen became almost as familiar with the oceans of the world as they were with their own backyards. They studied the lore of the tides and the winds, came to recognize the warning signs of uncharted reefs and unheralded typhoons, and learned where pirates were likely to lurk and how to fight them. In ports half a world away from home, they formed friendships which were to be valuable to them later.

During those twenty years, cabin boys of twelve or thirteen

advanced to be able seamen and mates and captains. Young men now, they were more at home on shipboard in the middle of a pathless ocean than on the streets of the little coastal towns where they were born. They learned the manners and customs and languages of faraway places, and were at ease in any company in any land. From their ranks were to come the famous clipper captains of the China run. In the meantime, other ships and other men were establishing the China trade.

2

The China Traders

━━━━━━━━━━━━━━━━━━━━━━━━━━━━━━━━━━━━

A definition of *trade* is "the exchange of goods for other goods or money." This sounds simple, but when the trade is taking place between people half a world apart in miles and many worlds apart in ways of living and thinking, it is not as simple as it sounds. In its early days, trade with China involved almost as many problems as trade with Mars would today. The actual distance to be crossed seemed almost as great and difficult to the people of that day, and the habits of the Chinese almost as strange to them, as the habits of the Martians would to us.

The ships could overcome the distance barrier. Once they were anchored in Canton Bay, however, there was still a wide gulf to be crossed. This was the gulf of strangeness between two groups who had very little in common, not language, ideas, beliefs, or customs. The chief thing they shared was the wish to exchange goods for profit. To make this exchange possible, someone must build a bridge of understanding across the gulf.

The ships' captains could not do it. They were men of action.

16

They might sail ships well, but they lacked the patience, business sense, and smoothness necessary to deal with the shrewd and baffling Chinese. Soon after Captain Green of the *Empress of China* opened the China trade, the big American companies sent out to the Orient their own trained representatives. They might be called purchasing agents, but actually they were much more than that. Because of the peculiar conditions in China, they had to be more than merely good bargainers.

Today we hear much about the Iron Curtain and the Bamboo Curtain which shut off various countries. They are nothing new, and they do not compare in completeness with the curtain that screened all China in the early days of the China trade. Somewhere behind this curtain was the Emperor, vague, all-powerful and mysterious, whose word was absolute law. He forbade "foreign devils," as people from the Western world were called, to set foot on the mainland of China. The Emperor was supposed to be above bothering his head with such crude matters as business and money. He was an intelligent man, however, who could see the advantages to China and to himself of a healthy foreign trade. He put affairs of commerce into the hands of a group of highly placed mandarins, or public officials roughly comparable to princes, called the Cohong.

The Cohong dealt directly with the Yankee traders and were part of the bridge across the gulf of strangeness. They were proud, honorable gentlemen who felt keenly that haggling and bargaining were unbecoming to mandarins. Therefore they used assumed names in the business world. Perhaps the most famous of them all, Wu Ping-ch'ien, was known, respected, and even loved all over the Western world as Houqua.

17

Hoqua was one of the most respected of the Cohong.

The mandarins had a difficult job. From the moment a foreign ship anchored at Whampoa, they were directly responsible to the Emperor for the behavior of all its crew. If any unfortunate incident occurred, a Cohong member was punished. In extreme cases he might forfeit his life. In less serious circumstances he would be forced to remove the mandarin's button from his tight, black skullcap, a disgrace very nearly as bad as death. But the profits made by trading with the Americans, British, Dutch, and others were enormous, and some of these Chinese merchants were probably the richest men in the world of their time.

The Cohong persuaded the Emperor to make one small exception to the rule that kept aliens out of China. On a narrow strip of swampy land along the Pearl River, in Canton, the "foreign devils" were allowed to build warehouses, showrooms, and offices in which to conduct business, and quarters in which to live. These were called "hongs," or "factories." There were thirteen of these foreign factories in a line facing the river. The American space was occupied by trading firms from Boston, New York, and Philadelphia. After a brig or an East Indiaman had come in and unloaded, the hongs were heaped high with tools from mills, piles of tin, iron, copper, and steel, bundles of seal, otter, beaver, and fox pelts, and sandalwood from the Sandwich Islands. Gradually these things disappeared behind the Chinese curtain, and the air of the hong became fragrant with the scent of cloves and nutmegs. Chests of tea and bales of silk replaced the tools and metals. Lichee nuts and kumquats, gingerroot and jade—the inventory of the hongs, for all its business nature, read almost like poetry.

Outside of business hours the life of the traders in the hongs was luxurious. An army of Chinese servants waited on them hand and foot, keeping their clothes pressed and mended, serving them sumptuous meals of shark fins, plovers' eggs, and octopus with subtly seasoned rice, and pampering them like princes. Yet the "foreign devils" were almost prisoners. Beyond lay the great and fascinating city of Canton, but the traders were not allowed to move past the cramped limits of the hongs except on special occasions.

Such an occasion might be dinner as the guest of one of the Cohong, when the Westerners observed with wonder the style in which the mandarins lived. Their houses had marble floors covered with silk and velvet carpets, the furniture was of richly inlaid or japanned wood, and there were rare and beautiful bronzes, porcelains, and paintings. Loveliest of all were the carefully landscaped gardens. Wherever one looked he saw a picture: a little waterfall leaping into a pool which reflected swans and ibises, a view of the countryside framed by an arched bamboo bridge, a peacock spreading its gorgeous tail on a marble terrace; and banks and pyramids of flawless chrysanthemums. The Chinese admired perfection. They planted their flowers in pots, and when a blossom began to fade, they replaced the pot with another at the peak of its blooming. Or all the pots were shifted and rearranged so that an entirely new and different effect was created. The meals partaken in these fairy-tale surroundings lasted for hours. Often, thirty courses were served on dishes of jewel-like fineness and rarity, and wines were drunk from tiny silver cups. The foreign traders felt almost as though they were visiting another planet.

The representatives of the companies were usually more than competent employees. They were younger members of the firms, or relatives of the owners—educated gentlemen who could meet on equal terms with the highly cultured mandarins. To send an ignorant hired hand to deal with a people who had invented gunpowder, paper, and the culture of silk would have been considered insulting. Some of these traders took to Chinese life like fish to water. John Perkins Cushing is a good example.

At sixteen, John was a clerk in his uncles' Canton office when the chief local representative became ill. John took over the running of the J. & T. Perkins Company hongs and proved so competent that his uncles put him in charge. He stayed in Canton for twenty years, piling up an immense fortune for himself, as well as for the owners. At last he retired home, but so in love was he with the Chinese way of life that he tried to take it with him. He surrounded his Boston house with an exquisite porcelain wall enclosing a garden in the Chinese manner, with lotus lilies, mandarin ducks, and harshly crying peacocks. The Cantonese servants he brought back to run his household continued to wear their native dress and their pigtails. They looked strange on the gray streets of staid old Boston.

Others of the traders were never completely happy in China. In spite of the luxury and color of the life, they were homesick. They missed the straggly autumn gardens of New England, the homely taste of baked beans, and the hiss of sleet against windowpanes. Most of all, they missed their families. Although the Emperor was resigned to permitting Western men to live on the fringe of Canton, he drew the line at their women. If a "foreign devil" wished to bring his wife, sister, or daughter with him, he might; but she would have to stay on the peninsula at Macao, sixty-five miles downriver.

Macao was a pretty little city, with white houses set like flowers among the terraced trees, and a lovely church rising above them all. There was a small Portuguese garrison, but the greater part of the population consisted of the families of the Canton traders. During the summer months the traders themselves came down the river to vacation with their wives and children. As soon as the new tea crop was harvested, however, they went back to business, which would keep them close to the hongs for the next five or six months, and their families were left to their own devices on Macao.

There was no lack of entertainment. The young Portuguese officers of the garrison were always ready to play tennis or to organize picnics on Green Island, just offshore. Often, officers of ships lately arrived in Canton Bay from America were rowed over to Macao to bring news and letters from home, and usually they stayed to dinner. There was horse racing at the Barrier, the wall beyond which foreigners could not go toward the mainland; and cricket matches among the English boys; and walks in the evening along the city esplanade, the Praya Grande. There were teas, and garden parties, and church bazaars. Since Chinese servants did all the chores, the women worked hard at filling their time with social activity. Although it may have seemed rather pointless, life on Macao was leisurely and pleasant enough.

From Macao, all the busy life of the Pearl River entrance could be observed. There might be a ship coming in from the Horn, bustling under her cloud of canvas, or a stately East India-

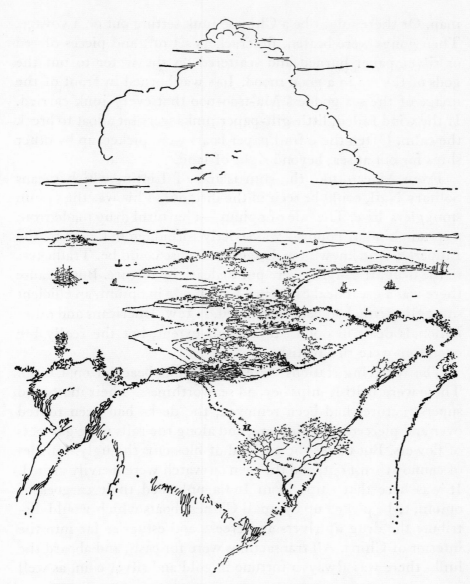

Macao was a pretty city overlooking the river entrance.

man. Or there might be a Chinese junk setting out on a voyage. Then gongs were beaten, firecrackers set off, and pieces of red or silver paper burned and scattered on the water to put the gods of the sea in a good mood. Joss was burned in front of the image of the sea goddess Ma-tsoo-poo that every junk carried. If the wind failed, little gilt-paper junks were set afloat to break the calm. Often these frail paper boats were picked up by other ships far out at sea, beyond sight of land.

From Macao, too, the slim island of Lintin, which means Solitary Nail, could be seen in the distance. This was the opium smugglers' base. The sale of opium—a harmful drug made from a certain kind of poppy—was strictly forbidden in China by the Emperor, who knew how dangerous its use could be. Traffickers in the drug, if caught, were put to death by torture. But because there was a great deal of money to be made in opium, an efficient smuggling ring had been organized. A few Americans and other nationals dealt in opium to a small extent, but the really big operators were the British.

The receiving stations were three hulks beached on Lintin. These were British ships beyond seaworthiness. Their masts and superstructures had been removed, the decks had been roofed over and pierced for chimneys, and along the rails were gay pots of flowers. But under the garland of blossoms the ugly muzzles of cannon thrust out, and the men on watch were heavily armed. It was here that ships from India unloaded their cargoes of opium, to be picked up by small Chinese boats which would distribute the drug up rivers and creeks and estuaries far into the interior of China. All transactions were for cash, and aboard the hulks there was always a fortune in gold and silver coin, as well

CANTON

FATI
GARDENS

HONAN

WHAMPOA ANCHORAGE

PEARL RIVER

THE BOGUE

CHUENPEE FORT

BOCCA TIGRIS

INNER CHANNEL TO MACAO

LINTIN BAY

HANGSHAN IS.

LINTIN IS.

KOWLUNG

LANTAO CHANNEL

LEMA CHANNEL

HONG KONG IS.

MACAO

GREAT WESTERN CHANNEL

LEMA IS.

| 10 | 15 | 20 | 30 | 40 |

STATUTE MILES

Canton and its approach.

as the valuable opium. The hulks were well guarded against raids by pirates.

Naturally, such open defiance of the law did not escape the Emperor's attention. He asked politely that the smuggling be stopped. When this failed, he ordered a captured Chinese smuggler to be publicly strangled in front of the British hong. The British were shocked, but not sufficiently to give up smuggling opium. Next, in 1839, the Emperor sent to Canton a tough police officer named Lin, with orders to seize and destroy all the opium he could find, no matter who owned it. Lin meant business. He forced the British to turn over to him six million dollars' worth of the drug, which he dumped into the river. He so frightened the British with his threats that they all fled to Macao. As soon as they were gone, mobs looted and burned the British factory.

Thus, in 1839, began what is known as the Opium War. Ships of the British Navy retaliated by shelling the Chinese forts guarding the mouth of the Pearl River, and regiments of the British Royal Marines marched inland, killing and destroying as they went. They arrived at Canton in time to rescue the American traders, besieged in their own hong.

At the end of the war, in 1842, a treaty was signed that completely changed the China trade. The island of Hong Kong, of enormous value, was given outright to the British, and five other ports, called "treaty ports," were declared open. They were Amoy, Foochow, Ningpo, Shanghai, and Canton. Now the traders were able to bring their families to live with them in these cities. Instead of dealing through the Cohong, they were allowed their own consuls to represent them with the Chinese government. As a further indication of change, no conditions about opium trading were made in the treaty. The British piously stated that "they hoped the smuggling would cease," but of course it didn't. The only difference was that now not much was said or done about it, and the drug traffic grew greater than ever.

The opening of more ports did turn the eyes of the world on the China trade more than ever before, however.

3

The Clipper Ships

Ever since colonial days, American shipbuilders had been working toward ever-increasing speed in their boats. The old broad-beamed, deep-keeled, rather tubby and clumsy vessels were slow, and they were ill-suited to run in and out of the shallow bays and narrow channels of the eastern coastline. As time went on, the men building boats in the little rivers and coves along the shore were likely to straighten out a line on the hull here, make the craft a little narrower there, crowd on a little more sail, at first experimentally, then from the knowledge that actual sailing brought. During the worrisome years of the American Revolution and later, during the War of 1812, when the British blockaded the coast and patrolled the seas, speed became a matter of life and death to American sailors. All up and down the coast sharp-hulled little schooners with pointed bows dodged in and out of harbors. And in the Chesapeake Bay, a slender, clean-lined type of boat with raking masts, called a

The Baltimore clippers were superb blockade runners.

"Baltimore clipper," proved itself supreme as a blockade-runner and privateer.

The many schooners and Baltimore clippers were fast, seaworthy, and easily handled, but they were small. Everyone agreed that they would be no use for long ocean voyages. They would founder in really big storms; and even if they didn't, they could not carry enough cargo to make long voyages pay. In 1832, a Baltimore merchant named Isaac McKim decided to have a big vessel built on the same general idea as a Baltimore clipper, but rigged like a ship.

When the *Ann McKim* was finished in 1833, she was a beautiful ship with long, easy lines and jaunty, raking masts. Her bottom was sheathed in copper, her decks gleamed with brasswork, and her trim was mahogany. She was pretty to look at, but no one believed for a minute that she was practical. Many sailors who saw her said she wasn't a merchantman at all, but only an overgrown schooner.

She made successful runs to South America and later to China, however, and true to McKim's reasoning, proved herself a demon for speed. But she still was too small to carry much cargo, and for some time other shipowners seem to have paid little attention to her. She may have given ship designers and builders something to think about, however. If the *Ann McKim* could sail halfway around the world speedily and without trouble, why wouldn't a much larger ship of the same general design do the same thing and show a good profit, besides? It seemed like good reasoning.

In 1843, the Howland and Aspinwall trading company of New York ordered the *Rainbow* built. She was 159 feet long,

Shipyard loafers ridiculed the Rainbow's *sharp bow.*

and only about 32 feet wide, with a sharp bow, shallow draft, and tall, slanting masts. While she was under construction, it was a favorite pastime of retired seamen, sailors ashore, and loafers who thought they knew something about ships to stand around criticizing the *Rainbow* and foretelling a sad end for her. If anybody aboard sneezed, they said, she'd never even get out of the harbor. She'd certainly never get out of sight of land, let alone to China. Looking at her sharp bow, curved inward instead of outward, they scoffed that it was "turned inside out."

She made the trip to Canton and back, ninety-two days out against the monsoon and eighty-eight days home. This established her without argument as the fastest ship in the world. By the time she arrived back in New York, her captain, John Land, was in love with her. Enthusiastically he described how the *Rainbow* "clipped down the wind." She was one of the earliest of the slim, narrow ships with clouds of sail which came to be known as "clipper ships."

The passion for speed and for setting records was not simply sporting rivalry. It was good, sound business. The quicker a ship got to China and back, the more trips she could take in a year and the more money she would make. More important still, the tea that made up a large part of every cargo lost its freshness and flavor if kept too long at sea. Being packed for a long period in a damp hold did not improve other merchandise, either. The ship that came first and fastest home from China commanded the highest prices for her well-kept cargo; and the laggards that limped in last from a slow voyage had to be content with whatever they could get in a market already swamped with tea, silk, spices, and other Oriental goods. Even one day cut off a voyage meant thousands of dollars gained. Speed was important to ship-owners, and naval architects tried to design faster and faster vessels.

Among the designers was a young man named Donald McKay. Until he was sixteen he had lived on a starved little farm on the Nova Scotia coast. The farm could not support the large family, and there was no work to be found nearby. He had scraped up passage to New York on a lumber schooner, there to seek his fortune. He arrived in 1826, friendless, almost penniless, and very much awed by the bustle of the big city. He had never been out of the backwoods before.

Instinct led him to the waterfront where the big shipyards were located. Back home, he and his brother Lauchlan had been forever repairing and rebuilding old boats that other people had abandoned as worthless. Boatbuilding had become his greatest interest, and he felt at home here where ships were being built. He found work as an apprentice, and gradually became an excellent shipwright—a carpenter and builder. And he kept his eyes and ears open, learning all he could about ships, and thinking and dreaming of ways they might be improved.

Two other young men of the time were thinking and dreaming about better ships, too. One was a young draftsman named John Griffiths, who had radical ideas about ship design; the other was Nat Palmer, who knew everything there was to know about how ships acted in all kinds of water and weather. These three carved out little models of their dream ships, drew plans and hull designs, and worked out complicated mathematical problems having to do with stresses and strains, and always with

33

speed. They studied the flight of birds and watched the fish and swimming waterfowl to see how they cut through the water.

These young men were all thinking along the same lines, and their ideas shaped the ships to come. It was John Griffiths who designed the *Rainbow*, and so proved that his ideas were right. Donald McKay became the foremost shipbuilder and designer in America, and so, the best in the world. And Nat Palmer, who had a continent named for him at twenty-one, rose to be one of the two or three top clipper-ship captains, known all over the globe.

A great deal of careful work went into building a ship. The vessel, for a long time, was just an idea in the designer's head and a collection of sketches and difficult computations on paper. When he felt sure that his calculations were right, the designer made a "lift model." This was a little wooden ship, small enough to be held in the hands, made in layers held together by pegs. The layers could be lifted off to show just how the ship would be built and what the dimensions would be throughout her entire depth. If the future owner of the ship—the man who had ordered it and was going to pay for it—approved this tiny model, a contract was signed and work on the ship itself could begin.

From the sections of the model, a plan of the ship was drawn to scale. The next steps took place in the mold loft. This was an enormous, well-lighted room with a black-painted floor. A copy of each of the lifts, blown up to the actual size of the ship, was drawn on the floor in chalk. Huge as the loft was, it was not large enough to hold all these plans separately. Because the drawings had to overlap each other, different colors of chalk were used. Soon the black floor was covered with a bright carpet

34

Patterns of the ship's sections were drawn on the floor of the mold loft.

of interwoven plans, utterly confusing to most people, but not to the experienced designer and his assistants. They now cut molds—thin pieces of straight or bowed wood—in the exact shapes of the drawings on the floor. These molds were the patterns to be taken to the shipyard, where the builders would follow them, much as a dressmaker follows a paper pattern.

It took months to build a ship. During this time, people stood around watching the work, just as groups today watch the construction of an office building. Everyone considered himself an authority, and opinions flowed freely as the ship took shape in the lumber-scented, hammer-loud air. But no one, not even the designer or builders, could really know how she would behave until she had been launched, and tested by the sea.

The launching of a clipper was a big event. When, in 1852, the *Sovereign of the Seas* was launched, for example, a public holiday was declared in the city of Boston. A huge crowd gathered at the bunting-trimmed yard, bands played, guns were fired, and speeches were made. Then the blocks that held the ship captive on the greased ways were knocked out. Slowly at first, then faster and faster, until the ways smoked from the friction, she glided into the water, tossing spray and foam in a great wave under her bow. Important guests were served a splendid champagne luncheon in the mold loft, and the carpenters, apprentices, and all who had helped build her enjoyed a generous feast—along with their families and friends—at tables made of trestles and planks set up outdoors in the yard. The whole community shared a feeling of pride in the famous ships built and launched within its boundaries.

After the launching, the ship was towed to another yard,

*The whole community celebrated the launching of
a clipper.*

where the intricate web of ropes and lines was rigged on her masts. The sails that had been made especially for her were brought from the sail loft and taken aboard. Now, at last, the dream in the designer's head was an actual object of wood, copper, and canvas, capable of traveling a world away.

No matter where an American clipper went, she was recognized. Nobody but the Americans made ships like these at first. The hulls of the American clippers were almost always painted black, with perhaps a line of gold or scarlet trim near the rail. They were long and slim, and streamlined as arrows. The decks were holystoned to whiteness, and the metalwork gleamed. Placed at the bow, where it breasted the seas, every ship had a figurehead, an expertly carved image—possibly a gilded dragon, or a mermaid with her arm outstretched, or perhaps a fierce eagle. Sometimes it was a likeness of the woman for whom the ship had been named. From the stern rippled the Stars and Stripes.

Rising from the narrow deck were the masts, taller than the ship was long, so tall that they seemed to overbalance the delicate hull. They were painted white, or cleanly scraped and varnished. Their slender strength supported great clouds of sail. In spite of high winds and heavy seas, American captains prided themselves on keeping as much canvas aloft as possible. That was the only way to make records. From the tallest mast streamed the house flag, the swallow-tailed or pennant-shaped insignia of the company that owned the ship. A clipper under sail was a splendid sight.

Getting ready for sea was a complicated task. Since the ship would not touch shore again for weeks, everything that could possibly be needed must be stored aboard. There must be drinking water and plenty of food, of course, and spare sails and ropes and spars in case of damage. Tools for repairs must be at hand, and medicines for illnesses, and suitable clothing for the hot tropics and for the frigid weather at the Horn. Then the cargo —woolens, furs, cotton, lumber, the ginseng root that the Chinese used extensively in medicines—must be secured in the holds so that it would not shift in rough seas. If the ship seemed to ride too high, ballast was added, usually pig iron which could be sold at the voyage's end.

Most of the preparation for sailing was done under the supervision of the mate, who was responsible to the captain. The captain himself had other duties to keep him busy until the clipper put to sea. He interviewed the owners, getting his final instructions. Often he went about town placing private bets on his ship, in the race to the Orient and back. He always took his chronometer and other instruments to a reliable man to have them checked. Before he reached home again, his ship, his cargo, and the lives of all aboard might depend on their accuracy.

The clipper captains were striking men. Nearly all of them were young, in their twenties or early thirties, and most of them swaggered a little as they walked down the street. They were proud of themselves and their position. Because they were sure of their reputations for being hardfisted and tough when necessary, they were not timid about dressing elegantly. They wore tall beaver hats, snow-white stocks and gloves, velvet cravats, and shiny patent-leather shoes. Their well-cut blue coats with big pearl buttons fitted superbly, and their light-gray pants were skintight. Heavy gold watch chains looped across their brocaded

A clipper captain was Somebody.

vests, and as they walked, they swung gold-headed ebony canes. A clipper captain was Somebody.

The mates dressed more quietly. Usually they wore good, but inconspicuous, dark suits ashore. They were careful about clean shirts and well-polished shoes, though, out of respect for the dignity of their position. No good mate planned to remain a mate all his life. He intended to be a captain as soon as possible. A neat, businesslike appearance would not only help in this ambition, but would impress the men under him, as well. Little matters like this aided discipline aboard ship.

In the British merchant marine, the crews wore uniforms. There was nothing uniform among the common American seamen. Unlike the British, who were much under the influence of the Royal Navy with its strict regulations, the American sailors were very independent. They wore whatever appealed to them and was comfortable and convenient. Their shirts were of blue, red, or green flannel, or of nankeen, a coarse, colored cotton fabric that came from China. Their trousers were of gray, black, or brown wool, or of another Far Eastern discovery that had proved practical, dungaree, the same blue material that is worn so widely today. The trousers were held up by suspenders, leather belts wide or narrow, or sometimes simply by a piece of rope. Headgear might be knitted caps, soft felt hats, or even a scarf worn like a turban. There was nothing "regulation" about the crews of the American clippers except their weather-bronzed faces, the fancy tattooing on their muscular arms, and the rolling gait with which they swung down a street. By these signs you could tell a sailor as far as you could see him.

Sailing day was bustling and busy. The mates were aboard

early, checking in the crew. More often than not, they had to go ashore and round up the men, who were having a last fling in the waterfront taverns. On British ships, rum was issued to the crews daily, but almost every clipper forbade alcoholic drinks aboard, except for a bottle of whiskey in the captain's medicine chest. The owners had found that a sober ship was a safer and more profitable ship, and they frequently paid the captains a bonus for keeping it so. Accordingly, the crews often celebrated while it was still possible.

The hour of sailing depended on the tide. When the time approached, the captain came aboard from his last errands ashore. Still in his resplendent shore clothes, he received a formal visit from the owners, come to wish him luck. After they had left, he went up the companionway and took his place of authority on the quarterdeck. Quickly he ran his experienced eye over the vessel, making sure that all was ready. Then he shouted to the mate, "All right, Mister!" The mate bawled an order, and the men sprang to the windlass that would warp the ship away from the dock.

"*As I was a-walking down Rotherhite Street!*" a voice began, and the whole crew joined in the chantey that timed their work and helped them haul:

> *Way, ho, and blow the man down,*
> *A pretty young creature I chanced for to meet,*
> *Give me some time to blow the man down.*

All along the shore, crowds cheered as the ship made sail and moved majestically down the harbor and out to sea. Fashionable ladies, ragged urchins, businessmen, and loafers all watched her until she became a pencil line of black beneath a towering, shining cloud of snowy canvas, and then just the glimmering suggestion of a cloud at the earth's edge, like a daytime moon. Then she was gone, vanished below the horizon, outbound for China.

4

The Flying-Fish Men

Once at sea, the ship's company quickly settled down to the routine it would follow for months to come. The modern short-cuts, the Suez and Panama canals, had not yet been built. To reach the Orient, it was necessary to sail down the length of the Atlantic, around Cape Horn at the southernmost tip of South America—or possibly around the Cape of Good Hope in Africa —and back up the Pacific. But in spite of the long absences from home, once sailors had tried the China trade, they seldom left it for the shorter packet runs to Europe or for short trips aboard coastal vessels. The Far East seemed to cast a spell that drew them back to it. Moreover, there was glamour attached to the "flying-fish" men, as the sailors who preferred the warm waters and the lands of the East were called. They were set apart from ordinary seamen—listened to with more interest, regarded with more admiration, treated with more respect. They deserved it. Exciting as their life certainly was at times, it was also and more often extremely hard and dangerous.

CHINA

CANTON
HONG KONG
FORMOSA

HAINAN

COCHIN
CHINA

LUZON IS.
MANILA
PHILIPPINES

MINDORO IS.

CAMBODIA

South China Sea

SPRATLY IS.

MALAY PENINSULA

MINDANAO IS.

SINGAPORE

BORNEO

Celebes Sea

HALMAHERA

DAMPIER ST.

E Q U A T O R

BANGKA

BILLITON

MOLUCCAS

CELEBES

MACASSAR ST.

CERAM

Banda Sea

NEW
GUINEA

SUMATRA

ANJER PT.
BATAVIA

JAVA

Java Sea

BALI LOMBOK IS.

FLORES IS.

SUNDA ST.

JAVA HEAD

CHRISTMAS IS.

Savu
Sea

SANDLEWOOD
IS.

TIMOR IS.

Arafura Sea

Timor Sea

Coral Sea

TO COCOS AND RODRIGUEZ IS.
AND
CAPE OF GOOD HOPE

AUSTRALIA

THE CHINA TRADE
SEASONAL ROUTES

MONSOON   xxxxxxxx
SPRING   ·············
AUTUMN   •••••••••
WINTER   ‒ ‒ ‒ ‒ ‒ ‒

Fortunately, the early days of a voyage—when the crew members were toughening up from their soft life ashore, and the ship and the men were learning to live with each other—were comparatively easy. The course lay south into warm, sunny weather. Being at sea again was new and pleasant. People had not yet begun to get on each others' nerves, as they would later on, from being cooped up together too closely and too long. And because there were still fresh meat and vegetables among the stores, the meals were good. Later, although there would be enough to eat, the fare would be monotonous. Without refrigeration, the cook would have to rely on salt beef and pork and such long-keeping vegetables as potatoes and turnips.

From the first, fresh water was used sparingly. The ship's carpenter was in charge of the water supply, which was contained in a huge iron tank holding between three and four thousand gallons. Each morning he pumped out into a barrel on deck, called the scuttlebutt, about one gallon for each person aboard. He reported the amount remaining in the tank to the chief officer, who entered it in the logbook, the daily record of the voyage. The cook and the steward took what water they needed for cooking and for the officers' quarters aft, and the men helped themselves from the rest as necessary. On hot days there were frequently several men around the scuttlebutt drinking and, naturally, talking. Thus the term "scuttlebutt" came to mean the idle talk exchanged at the scuttlebutt, and is still used to mean gossip or rumor.

The crew slept in the forecastle, pronounced fo'c'sle, a space below decks and in front of the mainmast. In ancient days, this was a damp, dark, badly ventilated hole, impossible to keep clean and comfortable. American clipper designers improved the fo'c'sle, dividing it into two sections so that each working shift had its own quarters, provided with hatches for light and air. How well the men fared here depended entirely on themselves. If they wanted to take pains, they would be snug and comfortable. If they were untidy and sloppy, they would probably be miserable. The matter was up to them. By methods of their own, experienced sailors usually saw to it that careless, dirty crew members mended their ways.

The officers' cabins were more elaborate, and the captain's cabin was really luxurious, with rosewood and mahogany paneling, and cushions on built-in seats. A captain sometimes took his wife and children along with him, and there might even be a piano in his quarters, on which the daughters of the family practiced their scales. The Colcord children of Searsport, Maine, practically grew up at sea. Young Joanna took her final high school examinations somewhere in the middle of the Pacific. Her mother had taught her every day from the books and assignments supplied by the teachers back home. The examination papers were mailed to Searsport from Hong Kong, and when Joanna returned home the next year, her diploma was waiting for her.

Once in a while a baby was born at sea, and his birthplace was known only by numbers taken from a navigation chart, such as Lat. 20° S., Long. 123° W. Many of the odd names handed down in New England families arose from the custom of naming the child after the nearest land: Java, Mindanao, or Ceylon. It is no wonder that so many of these children grew up with a passion for traveling and for the sea.

Although the captain always had absolute command, on this first part of the voyage the mate was usually in direct charge of the crew, except in emergency. He knew his business: disciplining the men and keeping as much sail on the ship as she would carry. As he walked the poop deck, his eye was constantly on the billowing expanses of canvas above him and on the crew busy about the housekeeping chores of the vessel. Sailors were paid to work, and the mate saw to it that they did. Besides the running of the ship, they were always smartening her up, holystoning her decks, touching up the paint, polishing the brass. Later on, there would be little time for these jobs.

Every ship carried a chanteyman, a sailor who, in addition to doing his regular work, could sing and who knew the words of a great many sea chanteys, or work songs. A good chanteyman, it was said, was worth four ordinary seamen. He set the time and rhythm for the men who worked together at their tasks. Sometimes the chanteyman sang old songs, and sometimes he made up new words as he went along. But the whole crew came in strong on the refrain, a repetition of one line that occurred frequently.

Some of the chanteys were short and businesslike, suitable for quick, brisk jobs. These were not especially tuneful.

> *A Yankee sloop came down the river.*
> *Hah, hah, rolling John!*
> *And what do you think that sloop had in her?*
> *Hah, hah, rolling John!*

One was really beautiful, however, and was never forgotten

48

The crew worked to the rhythm of chanteys.

by a flying-fish man once he had sung it in the loneliness of the empty sea. It was called "Shenandoah."

> *Oh, Shenandoah, I long to hear you.*
> *Away, you rolling river!*
> *Away, away, I'm bound away*
> *Across the wide Missouri.*

> *'Tis seven long years since first I seed 'ee.*
> *Away, you rolling river!*
> *Away, away, I'm bound away*
> *Across the wide Missouri.*

The crews were divided into watches, which worked in shifts, usually of four hours. During the balmy tropic nights when the ship was bowling along smoothly with all her sails set, the mate often excused from duty all except two men, the helmsman and a watchman. The helmsman stood at the wheel, checking his steering with one eye on the compass and the other on the spreading sails above him. The watchman had very little to do except to keep track of the time, so that he could call the men who would relieve him and the helmsman. He drifted about the ship, stepping carefully over seamen who were taking advantage of the fine weather to sleep on the moon-lit deck, seeing the mate's sturdy form on the bridge outlined black against the glittering wake, hearing the rustle of the sails above him and the soft whisper of water against the ship's sides. The beauty and the peace of nights like this were what he would remember later, what would draw him back to the sea with all its cruel hardships.

Life even in this delightful climate was not one long, happy holiday. The crews were a mixed lot. American ships did not as a rule carry a majority of native sailors, and the few Americans who shipped before the mast usually did not stay there long. They were intent on rising as high as their abilities allowed. Of the American ordinary seamen whom the earlier Salem ship *George* trained, for instance, forty-five became captains, and twenty-six, mates. The Yankee disposition was not satisfied with a common sailor's berth.

Among the crew were Spaniards, Frenchmen, Portuguese, Africans, Chinese, Russians, Italians, and Scandinavians. Some of them were excellent sailors and some were not. Some were landlubbers and some were troublemakers. The landlubbers had to be taught, and the troublemakers had to be shown who was boss. These jobs fell largely to the mates, who had only their toughness to rely on. The mate had his stern voice, his hard eye, his quick fists, and a belaying pin or marlinespike with which to maintain discipline, and he used them all. Harsh treatment was sometimes necessary, and the men understood that. The way to keep out of trouble, they knew, was to do their work and mind their own business.

Southward the ship flew. The equator was crossed, and men who had never been beyond that imaginary line were ducked in a canvas sail full of warm, sapphire sea water. Almost without realizing it, green members of the crew became quick and skillful at swarming aloft and handling canvas. Then the brilliant blue skies gave way to low, scudding clouds, and the

On balmy tropic nights the ship bowled along smoothly.

sparkling seas grew dull and gray. The air grew colder and colder, and snow flurries raced over the sullen water. The men who had come aboard unprepared for winter weather were issued, and had charged against their wages, warm clothes and oilskins from the slop chest, a sort of ship's store. Albatrosses and sea pigeons appeared, to wheel and cry after the vessel; and the ghostly corposant—or Saint Elmo's fire—an eerie light due to atmospheric electricity, flickered blue around the mastheads.

As the long, icy Cape Horn rollers came shouldering out of the fog and scud, the captain spent more and more time on the bridge. Even when he was below, even when he was asleep, his trained ear was alert. From the hundreds of little noises that a ship under full sail makes—the creaks and rattles, the squeaks and bangs—his ear picked out at once the one small, wrong sound that might foretell trouble. Instantly the captain was wide awake and on his feet, ready to meet the emergency before it became serious. He was being well paid to keep the ship out of trouble and bring her safely to China.

The young, swaggering captains did not sail for wages, but for a percentage of whatever money was made on the cargoes they carried. In addition, a section of the hold was assigned them for their private use. In it they could carry, free, goods bought with their own money and eventually sold for their own profit. Captains had opportunities to pick up all sorts of tips about markets, and often made a pretty penny investing in palm oil, coffee, nutmegs, or other cargo.

Often, too, the captains were permitted to own the dunnage —the material in which the ship's regular cargo was packed

53

to prevent its shifting and rubbing during the voyage. Shavings and straw could be used, and so could bundles of rattan and bamboo, bolts of dungaree and nankeen. These things could be bought very cheaply in China and sold for much higher prices at home. A sharp captain could make a great deal of money. Many men were able to retire while still fairly young, and to live the rest of their lives in ease.

They earned their pay. The full responsibility of ship, cargo, and men's lives was no light burden, and never was it heavier than when the ship approached Cape Horn. If a captain seldom appeared on deck in the smooth-sailing tropics, he made up for it now. Often he never went below for days and nights on end, but paced the bridge or slept fitfully in a chair lashed to the rail to prevent its being swept overboard. He ate what the steward brought him, cold hunks of hardtack and salt beef, and mugs of molasses-sweetened coffee, which was often cold, too. Sometimes, going round the Horn, it was unsafe or impossible to keep a fire going in the galley stove. Now the captain's clothes were never dry, and he was never warm. The men could go below occasionally for shelter from the knife-edged gales and stinging salt spray, but he stayed at his post. It was no fun being captain when the clipper was off Cape Horn.

Today, ships seldom round the Horn. Instead, in a matter of hours they pass from ocean to ocean through the Panama or Suez canals. It is hard nowadays to imagine the lonely horror of the sea off that dangerous and desolate cape. Day after day the vessel fought the wild seas and howling gales. Waist-high combers broke over the decks, and driven spray froze in an icy sheath on sails and rigging. The bitter cold numbed the

The crew struggled aloft in the howling gales.

hands of the men as they struggled aloft to secure the rigid canvas, and bit into their bones. The heavy masts and yardarms whipped and thrashed under the load of sail. Too often, men were snapped from the rigging and hurled into the sea, their screams lost in the roar of the winds and the crashing of the waves. Putting about to rescue them would have meant the loss of the ship and all aboard. Heartless as it seemed, they had to be abandoned for the sake of the others.

Even so, many ships did not survive. Over and over the records read, "Disappeared at sea," "Sunk in ice off Cape Horn," or as in the case of the famous *Rainbow*, simply, "Lost." The surprising thing is not that so many failed to make port, but that so many succeeded. Perhaps the most surprising story of all is that of the *Neptune's Car*.

The *Neptune's Car* was a big, extreme clipper, commanded by twenty-nine-year-old Joshua Patten. His wife Mary was with him. She was nineteen years old, a beautiful girl, and this was her second voyage. Trouble started even before the ship reached the Horn. The first mate was unreliable and insubordinate, and Captain Patten was forced to arrest him and lock him in the brig.

That winter was the worst on record at the Horn. Many competent shipmasters turned back to Rio de Janeiro when they saw how impossible conditions were. Captain Patten chose to go on, but the constant strain and unbearable fatigue of doing his own and the first mate's work aggravated an attack of brain fever. He lay helpless in his cabin, apparently dying, his sight and hearing gone, his mind wandering.

The second mate was a good seaman, but he knew nothing

about navigation. Young Mary Patten did. On her first voyage, to while away the long hours at sea, her husband had taught her the use of his instruments. It had been more or less a game for her, but she was quick and intelligent and had become an expert navigator. Now she took command of the *Neptune's Car*. There was no one else to do it.

It seems impossible that this young girl whom acquaintances described as quiet, gentle, and ladylike should fight the great clipper safely around the Horn. But that's exactly what she did, and brought the ship into port at San Francisco fifty-two days later. It was not a record run, but it was better than most. What is more, she kept her husband alive during this time through her careful nursing. The best captains of the day freely admitted that Mary Patten was as good as any of them. She was a real heroine.

Few ships that rounded the Horn did so without damage. Masts were broken, leaks developed, and rigging was carried away. As each ship limped into the calmer waters of the Pacific, these things were mended. A vessel could, in dire emergency, put into Valparaiso, on the west coast of South America; but this stop cost time and money. Most repairs were made at sea. Extra gear had been brought along, and every clipper carried carpenters, sailmakers, and blacksmiths. The tasks were difficult, but not impossible; and now that every day brought bluer seas and warmer weather, the hearts of the men lifted. Once again they had defeated the terrible Horn, and ahead lay the joys of shore leave in Hong Kong. They were flying-fish men, they told each other, and no sailors in the world were their equal.

Mary Patten brought the ship safely round the Horn.

That the captains and crews of other nations regarded the Yankees as insanely reckless, driving their slim-lined and fragile clippers relentlessly day and night through all kinds of weather, bothered the Americans not at all. "Yeah! Hey! Heave away!" they bawled lustily as they hauled the ropes and crowded on yet more canvas. "I'm a flying-fish sailor just in from Hong Kong!"

Once around the Horn, the clipper's voyage was by no means over. There were still thousands of miles to go across the Pacific, and risks to be run. Typhoons prowled the vast ocean, storms so sudden and violent that a ship could be swamped in a few moments. Even vessels as sensitive to the lightest breeze as the clippers could become becalmed, drifting aimlessly while food and water ran low. These dangers past, there was still the passage into the China Sea. The course took the clippers among beautiful, jade-green islands, past a hundred misty-purple headlands, any one of which might conceal a fleet of Malay pirate *praus*. The Malays were fierce and bloodthirsty fighters who hunted in huge packs. They might be beaten off a dozen times, but still they kept coming, swarming over the sides until no Yankee was left alive and the ship was theirs. If the clipper slipped past the lurking pirates, she still might rip out her bottom on the heads of coral that lay just beneath the surface. Any one of many disasters could still overtake a clipper that had weathered the Horn; but, said the flying-fish men, they'd make it—with luck. And they rapped on wood or crossed their fingers.

The sailors were superstitious. They had seen so many strange things that it was easy for them to believe that black cats or

59

going to sea on Friday brought bad luck to a ship. If rats left a vessel for no good reason, they knew beyond argument that on her next voyage she would sink with all hands, and they refused to sign on her. Years before, when a fortune-teller predicted disaster for the merchantman *Massachusetts*, three separate crews were hired before enough men could be found to sail her out to China. When she arrived, it was found that her entire cargo was ruined and that her timbers were rotten. She was sold at great loss to a Danish company, and her crew scattered. Ten years later, over fifty of them—young, healthy men—were dead. The record reads, "James Crowley, murdered near Macao; John Johnson, drowned at Whampoa; William Murphy, killed by Chinese pirates; Jeremiah Chace, died with the smallpox at Whampoa; Roger Dyer, overboard off Cape Horn," and so on to its grisly end. It is not much wonder that sailors believed in signs and trusted in luck.

Finally—partly through luck, perhaps, but certainly more through courage and superb seamanship—the clipper entered the broad reaches of Canton Bay. It sailed past Macao, and the narrow island of Lintin, and teeming Hong Kong, surrounded by a floating city of houseboats. There were other American clippers in the roadstead, and majestic British ships, and battered fur traders from the Canadian Northwest. Among them darted Chinese junks and lorchas and sampans, with eyes painted on their bows to help them keep their courses and spy out the devils of the sea; and scrambling dragons—long, slim boats with fifty oars to a side. Smiling laundry girls called "Washee-washee?" from gay little boats with bamboo decks and curtains at their cabin windows. Other girls with flowers

Ships of all nations lay in anchorage at Whampoa.

in their hair sculled egg-shaped water taxis through the busy marine traffic. Beyond, the rice paddies of the mainland stretched soft and green to distant, pale-blue hills, and the Pearl River meandered down from Canton, the City of Rams, miles away.

A pilot was taken aboard, a small, brown man with a pigtail. He stood behind the helmsman and gave him short, quick orders in pidgin English. Under only a foresail and a jib, the clipper moved cautiously up the busy bay and into Whampoa, the Yellow Anchorage, where ships of all nations lay in a great crescent.

Then the captain resumed command. It was his right to select his own mooring. He had sailed two oceans and rounded the Horn with scarcely a quiver, but now he was suddenly nervous. He knew that from the bridges of a hundred vessels the finest captains in the world were watching through their long glasses to see how smartly he could bring his ship into her narrow berth. He waited until the man at the wheel had her exactly where he wanted her. Then, at last, he shouted strongly to the mate, "Let go your anchor, Mister!"

The chain rattled, the heavy anchor splashed, and the clipper swung at rest in the calm, muddy water. The trip from half a world away was over.

5

The Unforgettable Ones

In a time that was perilous and romantic and in an occupation that made almost daily demands on courage and skill, nearly everybody came close to being a hero. But there were a few who, for one reason or another, stood out in this company of giants.

Captain Josiah Cressy of Marblehead was one of the ablest skippers afloat, and it was only natural that stories should grow up around his name. For one thing, his wife always sailed with him as navigator. Although she was a small woman who had trouble holding the heavy sextant steady enough to take a reading of the sun or moon, no one could surpass her in the complicated mathematics of navigation. Moreover, she had a disciplinary effect on the crew. The roughest deckhand was careful of his language when Mrs. Cressy was around. Her tongue was more to be feared than the mates' fists. But nobody could be kinder and gentler, if a man was ill or injured. The sailors loved Mrs. Cressy as much as they respected her.

Then, too, Cressy was the captain of the *Flying Cloud*, a clipper that captured the public imagination through her great beauty, her lovely, descriptive name, and her habit of breaking records. It was while Captain Cressy was sailing the *Flying Cloud* across the Indian Ocean toward home that he had a rather odd experience. He met a Canton-bound vessel and received from her some New York papers which, although several weeks old, were new to him. Here he read the startling information that he himself had died at sea several months before.

This was better luck than it sounds. It was the custom of crooked lawyers, in those days, to meet ships as they docked after their long voyages, and to try to find some disgruntled sailor who thought he'd been abused. Then a damage suit would be brought against the captain. Although it was seldom successful, the action might keep the captain ashore for weeks. This was a nuisance. Usually the company employing him found it cheaper to pay off the complaining sailor and his lawyer than to have their captain out of service. The whole thing was a swindle.

At the time of his supposed death, there was a warrant out against Captain Cressy for having relieved an inefficient mate of duty, thereby damaging his reputation—or so the mate and his lawyer were claiming. But when they read that their victim was dead, they dropped the suit. The captain, who lived many years longer, was saved a great deal of bother.

When clipper captains were discussed, the first two names to be mentioned were usually those of Nathaniel Palmer and Robert Waterman. Two men could hardly have been more unlike, and they came to be the classic examples of use and

64

misuse of authority. Other captains were measured against them as being "nearly as good as Nat Palmer" or "almost as bad as 'Bully' Waterman."

Captain Palmer—the same Nat Palmer who first sighted Antarctica—entered the China trade early. The dangerous business of driving ships back and forth across the globe suited his stubborn and fearless nature well. The firm of A. A. Low & Brothers, New York importers and exporters, considered him their best captain. He was big and he was tough, and he knew how to get the best out of men and ships. But—perhaps because he himself had once been an ordinary seaman—he treated his crews with rough consideration. Most captains swore at their men almost absentmindedly, thinking this the only kind of talk they could understand. Captain Palmer never did. Instead, he hurled down on the deck an old white beaver hat that he always wore at sea, stamped on it, kicked it, and cursed it in such violent terms that even hardened sailors shuddered. But to the men he was always crisply courteous.

Everybody loved Nat Palmer, as he was known all over the world. Houqua was his great and good friend, and when the Lows named one of their early clippers the *Houqua*, in honor of their Chinese associate, Nat Palmer was chosen to sail her. When he retired, the Lows called their finest ship of all the *N. B. Palmer* as a tribute to him. He was one of the earliest members of the New York Yacht Club, and the Stuyvesants' famous yacht, the *Palmer*, was named for him. When he died at the age of seventy-eight, "Captain Nat" was mourned everywhere by people of all walks of life and every color of skin. He was a great and good man. Very few ordinary citizens have

Captain Palmer abused his hat instead of his men.

commanded so much affection; and no other has had named for him a part of a continent, a clipper ship, and a champion yacht.

Robert Waterman was a different sort altogether. There has never been a man who could get so much out of a ship as he could; about that there is no argument. He first attracted attention when he was made captain of the *Natchez*. This was a clumsy old hooker built for coastal trade between New York and New Orleans and entirely unsuitable for the China run. However, her owners, Howland & Aspinwall, decided that she could make money for them in the tea trade, slow though she was. To their great surprise, Captain Waterman brought her home from Canton in ninety-four days, a record up to that time. So impossible did this seem that everyone believed Waterman had found a secret shortcut to the Orient.

The secret lay in the merciless way he drove his crews and his ships. Because of his harsh treatment of the men, he was called "Bully" Waterman, a name in which he seemed to glory. Nobody got any sympathy out of Captain Waterman. A man did better than his best—or else. Ships, too, outdid themselves under his command. He crowded canvas onto them far past the point of safety, and was said to have padlocked the halyards to prevent more cautious mates from taking in sail while he was below deck. Right or wrong, these methods got results.

Impressed by the *Natchez*'s performance, Howland & Aspinwall built a new, extreme clipper, the *Sea Witch*, especially for Captain Waterman. Under his command, she established records that were never broken. But there was something dark about her. When sailors saw her familiar figurehead, a gilded dragon with gaping mouth and coiled tail, they hid or shipped out on the first ship sailing, to escape being shanghaied into Waterman's clutches. He was known and wholeheartedly hated in every port that he touched.

At this distance in time, it is hard to tell how much of this hatred was deserved. Other captains who knew Waterman personally respected and liked him as a hard-driving man who never asked of others more than he was willing and able to do himself. In spite of his reputation, he never lost a spar or cost his company a single dollar in loss or damage. After his retirement to a farm in Fairfield, California—a town which he helped found—he was popular with his rural neighbors. All the ladies thought he was a sweet old lamb. Perhaps all the talk against this superb seaman rose merely from the grumblings of a few lazy incompetents. It is hard to tell now.

Others than sea captains made names for themselves during the years of the China trade. Possibly Lieutenant Matthew Fontaine Maury of the U.S. Navy contributed more to the world of seamanship than any other single man. Early in his career, in 1831, he had been made sailing master of the war sloop *Falmouth*, with orders to take her as quickly as possible into the Pacific. He was only twenty-four years old, and naturally he was anxious to make a good impression on his superiors. He tried to find books with information on winds, tides, and currents, which would help him make a fast passage around Cape Horn. No books had been written on the subject. This circumstance gave him an idea on which he brooded for the next twelve years.

When he was put in charge of the Depot of Charts and Instruments (later the National Observatory and Hydrographic Office) in Washington, he had a chance to put his idea into practice. It was very simple. He thought that all known facts about winds and currents all over the world should be collected and made into easily understandable charts. He sorted out and arranged what information he could find in old logbooks from United States warships, and then he went further. He had printed what was called *Maury's Log*. It was before the days of public surveys, but *Maury's Log* amounted to perhaps the first questionnaire. Any American captain who was willing to cooperate received a copy, and in return for filling it out faithfully he could have without cost Maury's *Wind and Current Charts* for his own use.

At the end of each year, each captain sent his completed log to Lieutenant Maury, who used the tremendous mass of new information to draw up more-accurate charts. Seated in his stuffy little office, he could see spread out before his mind's eye all the oceans of the earth. Studying the dry figures, he discovered a pattern of ocean currents, drifting across vast seas and sweeping strongly around the ends of continents. He learned when and where winds could be depended on to blow steadily in one direction, and where they were fitful and unreliable. He charted monsoon and typhoon areas, and belts of doldrums and calms. All this knowledge he passed on to shipmasters through his charts, so that they were able to avoid dangers and take advantage of favorable conditions. The charts proved so valuable in practice that soon merchant ships of all nations were recording almost hourly observations of winds and currents in their *Maury's Logs*, and the Dutch and British navies carried them on all their vessels.

Beyond his small salary, Matthew Maury never made any money out of all this work, but Austria, Italy, Sweden, Prussia, Spain, and several other countries bestowed honors upon him and decorated him with special medals. More satisfactory to Maury, however, was the knowledge that seafarers everywhere knew his name and thought of him warmly as their personal friend and benefactor.

George Chinnery never designed or sailed a ship, made a chart, or traded a chest of tea. Nevertheless, it is through his work that we know best some of the ships and people involved in the China trade. He was a fat, homely little man, peering squint-eyed at the world through steel-rimmed spectacles; but he could paint like an angel. Although he was born in London, had lived in Ireland, and was a member of the Royal Hibernian Academy, some tragedy in his life cast him up on the shores of China. He lived out the rest of his days and died in Macao, a lonely figure whose chief interest was his painting.

In Chinnery's brilliant canvases we see Whampoa when all the tea fleet swung at anchor, and the ordered beauty of a mandarin's formal garden. His portrait of Harriet Low, a sister of the Low brothers who spent four years in Macao, explains why all the unmarried men from the Canton hongs paid court to this beautiful, spirited young woman. The noble, sensitive face of Houqua gazing thoughtfully from a Chinnery painting makes us understand the esteem in which he was held by men of the Western world who had nothing in common with him but honor and integrity. We owe Chinnery much.

70

They're gone now: Chinnery with his brushes and oils, Maury with his figures, all the brave captains and the lovely ships, all the nameless and faceless men who worked them back and forth across the globe in fair weather and foul. All that is left is a memory of the time when our country was younger and everything shone in the clear light of youth and daring— a memory to be cherished.

Through the China trade, a great many Americans became wealthy, and an army of others found work in designing, building, and sailing the clippers, and in manning the warehouses of America and the hongs of Canton. But these were not the most important benefits. There were others less easy to place a price on, but of greater and longer-lasting value.

In the Marine Museum at Searsport, Maine, there is a dim old photograph which suggests what some of these things might be. It shows a large group of people posed rather stiffly on the deck of a clipper. There are big, bearded men in captains' dress uniforms; women wearing feather-trimmed hats, lace mitts, and bustles; little boys in sailor suits with wide white collars; and little girls whose skirts are as long and whose expressions are as prim as their mothers'. The picture was taken, the faded writing underneath explains, on a long-ago Fourth of July, when nine American clippers lay at anchor in Canton Bay. The families of the officers of all the ships were old friends from back home. They had joined to give a party in celebration of the day, just as they ordinarily would have done had they been in America.

But these were not ordinary people. These men were as familiar with a hundred ports and thousands of people all over

They were entertained by kings with gold rings in their noses.

the seven seas as with their own streets and Yankee neighbors at home. To them, nothing was outlandish and nobody was queer. Their tolerance was as broad as their travels. These women had been entertained by kings with gold rings in their noses, a dozen wives apiece, and bodyguards of fifty almost-naked warriors. When they returned to their native land, they would have more interesting things to talk about than the price of eggs or the puddle on Main Street. They were American women, but they were also women of the world, with a sound understanding of world affairs.

These children were experts in geography. They knew where Manila was and what Borneo exported, because they had been there and seen for themselves. They had picked up cat's-eyes shells on the beaches of Java, seen Diamond Head outlined against the dawn, made pets of myna birds and mongooses. The little boys could do complicated mathematical problems, because their fathers had taught them navigation. They saw some sense and use in arithmetic. The little girls could change dollars into rupees or pesos or yen without thinking twice, because they had shopped with their mothers in odd corners of the world; and they knew what to say to a British admiral and how to ask directions in Portuguese or Hindustani or Dutch. They would never feel less than at home in the world.

Tolerance, understanding, poise, and wide knowledge—these are the truly valuable things that the China trade gave to those who were engaged in it.

6

The End of the Clippers

In 1849, two entirely disconnected events occurred. Gold was discovered in California, and the British repealed their old Navigation Laws. Although the effects of neither of these happenings was felt immediately, together they did hasten the end of the clipper-ship era.

By repealing the old, narrow laws which restricted British trade to specified countries and forbade ownership by Britons of any but home-built vessels, England opened up the whole world to her merchant marine, and opened her ports to American ships. Now the clippers raced between England and the Orient, always sure of a cargo, while the slower English ships moldered in the Chinese harbors, out of favor. Englishmen, eyeing the clean-lined American vessels, were appalled at what might happen to English shipping—but not for long. Very soon they, too, were building clippers to take the place of their slower ships, and the Americans were being given a run for their tea and silk money.

The first effect of the California gold rush was to create a demand for more and more fast ships. Everybody was bound for California, where there were no farms to furnish food, or herds to supply meat and dairy products, and no factories to make tools and clothes. All the necessities to keep the gigantic migration of gold-seekers alive had to be shipped around the Horn. Freight rates soared, and a fortune could be made on a single voyage to the West Coast, where prices were ridiculous. Corned beef brought $60.00 a barrel; sugar, $4.00 a pound; playing cards, $5.00 a pack; rough leather boots, $45.00 a pair; and common tin dishes, $7.50 apiece. Naturally the ship-building industry boomed, to take advantage of this inflation.

The trouble was that eventually too many ships were built and not enough able seamen could be found to sail them. Totally inexperienced hands signed on, simply to get to the goldfields. They were worthless when it came to handling a ship in Cape Horn seas. And the minute they landed in San Francisco they deserted for the diggings, leaving the ship not yet unloaded and often not even waiting to collect their pay. The waterfront was lined with ships rotting at their moorings for lack of crews to sail them away.

By 1855, the rush to the California goldfields was over. Moreover, many of the settlers in the new territory had turned from gold to farming. Much of the food needed could now be homegrown; a good part of the clipper cargoes was no longer necessary. Freight rates tumbled.

Many of the Californians had gone overland in covered wagons. As the size and richness of the country was revealed on these travels, the thought and energy of the nation grad-

75

ually turned away from the sea to the land, away from ship-building to the building of roads and railroads. Why should Americans sail to the ends of the earth, when they had their whole West to open up and settle? So began the decline of the clipper fleet.

Then, in the 1850's, the British, who had not been napping while the Americans were chasing gold, began to build a kind of vessel altogether different from any known before: iron steamships with screw propellers. Steam was not new. It had been used for quite a while on the New York-Liverpool packet runs. But the packet ships had been wooden, with paddle wheels for propulsion.

All the old clipper-ship masters were shocked. Sail was the only safe source of power, and wood was the only safe material for hulls, they claimed. These ridiculous iron boats of the British would surely blow up or sink. Steam was dangerous, and everyone knew that iron would not float.

Nevertheless, the new-fangled boats sped to and fro across the oceans in less and less time, and the old clippers began to gather barnacles in their berths. They had outlived their usefulness. When the Suez Canal, between the Mediterranean Sea and the Indian Ocean, was opened in 1869, making it no longer necessary to go the long way around Africa or the Horn to China, and cutting the time of a voyage in half or less, even the diehards gave in and changed to steam, or retired to a life ashore. They, too, had outlived their day.

But the vanished clippers had served their purpose. They answered the need for faster transport in a world where life was suddenly moving at a more rapid pace, and closed frontiers

76

were opening. They bridged the gap between the centuries when slow, clumsy sailing ships might spend months on a journey, and modern times, when sleek, streamlined motor vessels cross the ocean in a matter of days.

Index

81